LITTLE BIG BOOK
PLUS

Table of Contents

Meet
Margaret Miller

The children in Margaret Miller's books are all friends of hers. Ms. Miller says, "Taking photographs teaches you to see in a special way. I especially love photographing children."

MY FIVE SENSES

BY MARGARET MILLER

HOUGHTON MIFFLIN COMPANY

BOSTON

ATLANTA   DALLAS   GENEVA, ILLINOIS   PALO ALTO   PRINCETON

For my mother,
who always encouraged me to see

AUTHOR'S ACKNOWLEDGMENTS
My special thanks to the children in this book:
Miranda Berman, Annie Bernard, Rafael Espaillat,
Max and Gus Halper, Gideon Jacobs, and Morgan
Means.

—M.M.

Acknowledgments

For each of the selections listed below, grateful
acknowledgment is made for permission to
excerpt and/or reprint original or copyrighted
material, as follows:

Text

1 *My Five Senses,* by Margaret Miller.
Copyright © 1994 by Margaret Miller.
Reprinted by permission of Simon & Schuster
Books for Young Readers, Simon & Schuster
Children's Publishing Division. **25** "Ayii, Ayii,
Ayii," from *Songs of The Dream People: Chants
and Images from the Indians and Eskimos of
North America.* Edited by James Houston.
Copyright © 1972 by James Houston. Reprinted
by permission of the author. **28** "Look
Closely," from *Sense Suspense: A Guessing
Game for the Five Senses,* written and
illustrated by Bruce McMillan. Copyright ©
1994 by Bruce McMillan. Reprinted by
permission of Scholastic, Inc.

Illustrations

25–27 Maureen Zimdars.

Photography

i Banta Digital Group. **ii** Courtesy of Margaret
Miller (tl, tr, bl); Banta Digital Group
(background).

Houghton Mifflin Edition, 1997
Copyright © 1997 by Houghton Mifflin
Company. All rights reserved.

Printed in the U.S.A.

ISBN 0-395-80432-9

3456789-B-98 97

I have two eyes, a nose,

a mouth, two ears, and two hands.

With my eyes I see myself,

my shadow,

my dog,

and my city.

With my nose I smell popcorn,

a horse,

flowers,

and garbage.

With my mouth I taste watermelon,

the ocean,

medicine,

and ice cream.

With my ears I hear my baby brother,

a fire engine,

my piano,

and whispered secrets.

With my hands I feel finger paints,

sand,

water,

and a rabbit.

With our five senses, we enjoy our world.

AYII, AYII, AYII

an Inuit chant

Ayii, ayii, ayii,
My arms, they wave high in the air,
My hands, they flutter behind my back,
They wave above my head
Like the wings of a bird.

Let me move my feet.
Let me dance.
Let me shrug my shoulders.
Let me shake my body.

Let me crouch down.
My arms, let me fold them.
Let me hold my hands under my chin.

translated by James Houston

Look Closely
by Bruce McMillan

SENSE SUSPENSE
A GUESSING GAME FOR THE FIVE SENSES
Bruce McMillan

English		Español
I see	👁	Yo veo (YO VAY•o)
I touch	✎	Yo toco (YO TOE•co)
I smell	👃	Yo huelo (YO WELL•o)
I taste	👅	Yo saboreo (YO sah•bor•RAY•o)
I hear	👂	Yo oigo (YO OY•go)

28

Can you guess what these things are?

1

3
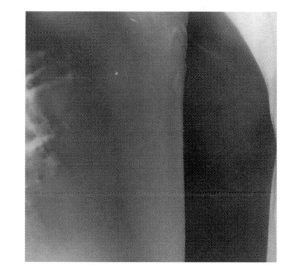

2

4

Here are the same things.
Are you surprised?

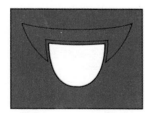

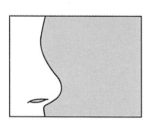

1

3

2

4